From Wed to Widow

A Guide to Self-Care, Self-Love, and Self-Discovery

DR. SHELLEY MCKINLEY

D1286591

MYND
MATTERS

Published by Mynd Matters Publishing
715 Peachtree Street NE
Suites 100 & 200
Atlanta, GA 30308

Books may be purchased in quantity and/or special sales
by contacting the author.

ISBN 978-1-953307-44-6 (Pbk)
ISBN 978-1-953307-45-3 (Hdcv)
ISBN 978-1-953307-46-0 (Ebook)

FIRST EDITION

*To the memory of my husband and to my sons,
parents, sister, extended family,
and longtime friends,
you experienced this journey with
me...sometimes pushing and sometimes pulling
me through.
I love you all!*

CONTENTS

FINDING STRENGTH

With certainty, life will throw you a curveball or two and unfortunately, you'll likely get hit by a few of them. Some may even knock you down—hard and fast, and you will have to make split-second decisions as to whether you'll get back up again. I have dealt with curve balls all my life, even when I was too young to recognize them, so I wear the badge of resilience. The biggest curveball proved itself worthy of the term as it came out of nowhere and shook my entire foundation.

It was a Tuesday morning and I was driving to Brownwood, Texas for work. My cell phone rang and when I answered, I was told my husband was found in the driveway and the ambulance had been called. Then, a paramedic got on the phone to ask me about Marvin's medical history. His hurried questions were met with confusion and shock. Minutes later, they confirmed what my heart feared. While they tried to save his life, their efforts failed. My husband was gone and my life was forever changed.

In a split-second, I became a widow. When you get married, you have time to plan a wedding and, in most cases, when you become a mother, you have nine months to prepare. When you become a widow, there is no luxury of time. The grieving process becomes secondary to planning a funeral and managing the "business" of death. Yet grief, and all the emotions that come with it, remain just below the surface.

Prior to that day, I spent my life often existing in states of denial. I was a master of stifling my voice and feelings. However, my husband's death was something I could not deny. It was something I could not simply pretend did not happen. I had to acknowledge he was gone, accept it, plan a funeral, and handle varied sorts of business that took on the speed of falling dominoes. I added a stripe to my resilience badge.

You may not have issues with denial but riding the wave of emotions associated with grief will put you in new and unfamiliar territory. The goal of this book is to give you small glimpses of the wave so when it comes your way, you will recognize it and have useful strategies that allow you to experience your feelings without repressing them. Ultimately, you have to go through a storm to get to the other side.

From Wed to Widow is intended to be a slow read. Anytime a scripture is mentioned, you should read it and meditate on it for a while. Ask yourself:

1. *How is my situation like the one described in scripture?*
2. *What is this saying to me? What hidden gem is here for me to find?*

So, how do you meditate? First, choose a place that gives you total peace. I have several. In my home, there is my bedroom and my backyard. If I am in my bedroom, I close the door and turn off the television. Occasionally, I play soft binaural beats because they are instrumental and lack a true melody.

If I am in my backyard, I sit in my chair between two trees, listen to the sounds of nature, and put my bare feet on the ground to engage all of my senses for a few minutes. Once I am centered and feel peaceful, I think about what I've read and allow my thoughts to answer those two questions. Finally, I journal whatever else comes to mind.

Early on, I realized the importance of creating a safe space beyond my home. For instance, one of the first things I do when starting a new job is find the nearest open chapel. It's for especially hard days when I need to get away immediately and connect with God. The times when I am too far away from home to get to my bedroom or my backyard. When those days come, I'll go to the chapel for lunch or right after work and just sit and pray. Afterwards, I sit in silence until my strength and peace are restored. Keep in mind, tears may flow, which is to be expected and accepted.

Suggested meditations are also included throughout these pages. Even when we are not dealing with scripture directly, meditation is helpful and an invaluable tool. So please take time to get centered and think on the suggested mantras. Do not feel inclined or required to finish within a specific time period.

ACTIVATING YOUR
MUSTARD SEED

L et me start by saying that I am not a biblical scholar. I am a widow who turned to the Bible to get me through some of my darkest days and ultimately, into my current state which is one of maintaining my sanity and committing to prosper in every area of my life. It isn't until things happen that you realize the purpose of some of your previous experiences. My formal education was spent in Christian schools at various times in elementary and again in high school. At the time, I did not appreciate my daily Bible study classes but have leaned on them ever since.

Prior to my husband's death, I spent little time on social media. When he died, I thought it was the fastest way to get the word out about his funeral arrangements, so I posted the details on Facebook. Since then, I have remained active on Facebook, Twitter, and Instagram. Repeatedly, I have seen new young widows making those same announcements and expressing pain through questions like, *Why, God, why?* and *What am I supposed to do now?*

I asked those questions, too, and often find myself still feeling those initial fears when faced with new dilemmas that I know we would have handled together. Most of those predicaments pertain to finances, our sons, and extended family relations. However, each time, I come back to Isaiah 54.

> *Fear not, you shall not be put to shame; you need not blush, for you shall not be disgraced. The shame of your youth, you shall forget, the reproach of your widowhood, no longer remember. For he who has become your husband is your Maker; his name is the Lord of hosts; Your redeemer is the Holy One of Israel, called God of all the earth.*
> *– Isaiah 54: 4-5*

I became a widow on April 24, 2018, at the age of forty-eight. I had dated Marvin for five years followed by twenty years of marriage. At that point, I had been with him for over half of my life so immediately I went into denial. As I talked to the paramedics on the phone before he was pronounced dead, I could envision ending the day sitting in a hospital room while he slept and recovered. Once he was confirmed dead, I imagined being in a bad dream unable to wake up. It was all too overwhelming and unfair. I needed to tell my two sons that their father passed away and attempt to manage their emotions.

I usually look for scripture during difficult times, but as the paramedic spoke, I could not focus enough to make meaning of what was happening. My sister shared Isaiah 54 with me and the entire chapter has helped me since then. But I immediately latched on to the words, *for he who has become your husband is your maker*. Every time I have to do things I would normally do with Marvin, I remember God is my husband now. He will be your husband, too.

There is comfort in knowing God is your husband. If your earthly husband could provide for you, protect you, cherish and love you, imagine how much more intentionally and intensely God can do these things for you, too? If you could believe in your earthly husband's ability to achieve these things for the betterment of your family, just imagine what God can do!

As a young widow, you face several mountains. You may ask yourself, "How am I going to sustain my lifestyle?" or "How can I shepherd my children through this tumultuous time in our lives?" or "How can I manage our finances?" The good news is you do not have to do it alone. God, as your husband, is with you, but he also sends other people into your life to meet these needs.

Of course, one of my first questions was, "How am I going to provide for us?" At the time of Marvin's death, my oldest son was a sophomore in college and my youngest was a senior in high school. Immediately, my mind raced to paying two college tuitions and maintaining my home. But guess what? The Bible had an answer for that, too.

In 1 Kings 17:4-24, God instructed the Prophet Elijah to go to a widow for his food, shelter, and other necessities. The text suggests that the role of the widow was to help Elijah. However, when I read the scripture, I believe God sent Elijah to the widow to help her. God could have sent Elijah to anyone for help, but he chose a widow who was so desperate and poor, she was planning to feed herself and her son their last meal then lay down and die. Yet, her flour and oil never ran out. In fact, when her son got sick, Elijah was able to heal him, too. Can you imagine how devastated this widow would have been if her son died, too? God saw into her future and sent her help before she even needed it. Have faith in the Lord and confidence in yourself to accept the help when it comes.

One of the first challenges I had to deal with involved my taxes. When God sends people into your life to help you, the first thing you must do is be honest with them. This requires the same vulnerability you reserved for your husband. If you think of your life as a television show, we all have scenes that get edited out when we tell the story. They aren't necessarily secrets, but they are not common knowledge either. God sent an excellent accountant into my life, but I had to disclose very sensitive information to him. Issues I purposely ignored, because my husband handled that aspect of our lives, were now mine to face and overcome.

Telling my truth was not shameful. I was not disgraced. I had lots of fear prior to telling the accountant the details of my situation, but guess what? The Earth didn't crumble, and life went on. AND I had a tremendous weight lifted off my shoulders. Fear tells us to expect bad things to happen when we tell our truth. Yet, we gain freedom, empowerment, and strength when we do so. As I said, I lived in denial so sharing my truth with others has happened countless times since then and each time, I am amazed at how freeing it is.

It is refreshing to know we can stand on God's promises. The word *shall* implies the promise. God tells us we shall not be put to shame or disgraced. Therefore, get the help you need. Shortly after getting financial help, I also got counseling from a licensed therapist. You may need help with your finances as I did or help with your children. Whatever help you need, pray to God to send it to you. And when He does, do not hesitate to be open and express your needs.

In your marriage, you were a team so you might feel that speaking your truth somehow disrespects your husband's memory. Talk about vulnerability! Whew! God knows you were a team, so understand that you are not shaming or disgracing your husband either.

Before you continue, read 1 Kings 17: 4-24. Who has God sent into your life to help you?

INTRODUCING: ANGER

Anger is one of the stages of grief, and once I moved from denial to anger, I seemed to stay there. It also did not help that I could not seem to catch a break.

Marvin had a trucking company, and although he had lots of equipment, he still leased the land where he kept everything. The owners of the land lost it to foreclosure, so all of his equipment had to be moved within two months of his death. Between my husband dying and moving trucks and trailers, was prom and graduation for my youngest. My sons were also suppressing their own grief and trying to stay strong for me, but those suppressed feelings were manifesting themselves in other areas of their lives. Needless to say, I experienced overwhelm and just wanted to curl up in a ball on my bed under the covers and never come out. I got mad that all of this was happening to me and I stayed mad! I was mad that I was alone.

Then I read 2 Kings 4: 1-7. It validated my anger and let me know I was okay in expressing it. When the widow approached the Prophet Elisha, I imagined her tone may have sounded like mine. She said, "MY husband, YOUR servant, is dead. You know he was a good God-fearing man, yet now HIS creditor has come to TAKE MY two children as HIS SLAVES."

Whew! That sentence is loaded with problems:

1. She didn't have the money to pay off the creditor before her husband died so you know she doesn't have it now.
2. The creditor is badgering her for the money.
3. The widow needs to save her children.

With my biblical imagination, I am 99% certain she was angry. Hopefully, you are not facing the amount of problems the biblical widow or I had. Elisha's advice to the widow was to identify what she had in the house and sell it. She was instructed to use the money to pay off her creditor and live on the rest. This guidance helped me, too. I needed to move trucking equipment in a short amount of time. Mind you, I did not have a CDL (commercial driver's license) and had no clue what to do. However, like before, God sent me help in the form of people. When I assessed my situation, I could move the equipment and continue to pay for storage fees, or I could sell it. I chose to sell it all. Once I made that decision, God sent me help and buyers.

God sent two men I did not have to ask for help as well as a mother of the church who came every evening with her son. Just having her present was beneficial to avoid the dynamics with the men being perceived as flirtatious. God sent me exactly who I needed and when. Your first decision will be different from mine, but it will require you to lean on God. What are you struggling with today? Give it to God and He will work it out for you.

Money met my immediate need, but it did not remove the anger. Intense anger lasted at least one year and still comes back occasionally. My anger did not subside until I started seeing my therapist. My anger caused my neck and shoulders to hurt constantly, and I was always irritable.

One day, a coworker suggested I go to her massage therapist. Without hesitation, I went the same day during my lunch break. Although it helped temporarily, an hour or two later, the pain and cramp returned. After a few weeks, she asked if I had ever considered seeing a psychotherapist. I lashed out at her, saying, "I don't want people in my business!" She replied calmly in a nurturing tone, "It's not about them, it's about you." Somehow, the way she said it let me know I NEEDED therapy. I called my employee assistance program and asked for a Black woman in my zip code. My request was specific because I didn't have the mental and emotional bandwidth to explain my cultural or religious nuances and assumed a Black female therapist would understand me better. I also didn't want to drive far.

Marvin died in April 2018 and I started seeing a therapist in August of that year. During my first session, she asked, "Do you know why you're here?" I yelled, "I know exactly why I'm here! I'm angry!" She had an intern sitting in my session, so she had us stand back to back, and told me to talk to that intern as if I was talking to Marvin. I did not stop yelling and crying until my hour was over. Again, I give God the glory! Without any research on my part, he led me to the exact therapist who could handle my anger and help bring me out of it. He also used my coworker to point me in the right direction.

Leaving the anger behind and moving more toward acceptance has been hard, ongoing work. I want to introduce you to a few biblical people that also have given me great lessons in how to move forward. I go back to their stories often, and each time I read them, I get new insight. They will serve as a foundation for the topics that lay ahead of us.

LESSONS FROM WIDOWERS
AND WIDOWS OF THE BIBLE

Jacob / Israel
Genesis 35: 19-21 Jacob becomes Israel

Thus, Rachel died; and she was buried on the road
to Ephrath [that is Bethlehem]. Jacob set up a
memorial stone on her grave, and the same
monument marks Rachel's grave to this day. Israel
moved on and pitched his tent beyond Migdal-eder.

For twenty-five years, I was half of "Shelley and Marvin." As I said, I was forty-eight years old and had been with Marvin over half of my life. Therefore, we had a collective identity.

As days and months pass after your spouse's death, you will get sharp reminders that you are an individual, no longer part of a couple. My reminders came in the form of filing my taxes for the first time as a widow. It came again when I had to mark widow on my sons' FASFA forms. These unexpected incidents that occur where you are required to declare or change your marital status can be unnerving and plummet your good mood to a dark place.

I listen to Dr. Jasmine Sculark, Dr. Jazz, as she is affectionately known, often and I encourage you to do the same. When I heard her preach about Jacob burying Rachael and leaving as Israel, it resonated with me deeply and caused me to go to that scripture for further study. For me, that scripture told me I needed to accept my new identity and keep moving forward. Whether you like it or not, you will have to craft a new life and a new identity. To accept a new identity, one of being an unmarried woman, you have to reassess the goals and aspirations that you formed as a couple and ask yourself, *Are these still MY goals and MY aspirations?* It isn't easy to do but it has to be done.

Two chapters prior to Rachel's death, God had given Jacob his new name. However, I am sure his wives and children still saw him as Jacob and still called him Jacob. I could relate because I became Dr. Shelley McKinley in 2011, seven years before Marvin died. That title was something I had to grow into and was one that was not used by my husband, my children, or my extended family and friends. Like me, who still referred to myself as Shelley, in my biblical imagination, it is likely that Israel still called himself Jacob. It is clear, however, that he left the burial site as Israel, the originator of twelve tribes.

We all leave the burial site of our spouses as a changed person. In my marriage, I was somewhat naïve and usually extremely optimistic. I always chose to see the bright side of situations because Marvin often took on the hard stuff. In fact, sometimes he would say, "I need you to take your rose-colored glasses off for ten minutes and listen." I didn't have the luxury of wearing my rose-colored glasses anymore. I was filled with anger over my situation and had to fight against that emotion to even begin to accept my new individual identity. Denial and anger are natural stages, but you can't stay there. Yes, you are grieving, but think of it as living <u>with</u> grief, not living <u>in</u> grieve. There is a difference.

Genesis 35:27

Jacob went home to his father Isaac at Mamre, in Kiriath-arba [that is, Hebron], where Abraham and Isaac had stayed.

You may find, as I found, the suggestion to widows throughout the Bible is to go home to your family. Losing your husband is like taking a gut punch that knocks you to the floor. You want to stay there on the floor, curled in the fetal position under a heap of covers, however, you cannot. The demands of life will not let you do that. I believe we are told to return to our families because we are not at our best emotionally and we need to be with people who have our best interests at heart. Home and family are loose terms that we will discuss further later.

<u>Tamar</u>
Genesis 38: 11

> *Then Judah said to his daughter-in-law Tamar,*
> *"Stay as a widow in your father's house until my*
> *son Shelah grows up" – for he feared Shelah also*
> *might die like his brothers. So Tamar went to live*
> *in her father's house.*

I was doing extensive travel for work at the time of Marvin's death. In fact, I was driving for business when I got the call that he had collapsed in the driveway. Initially, I thought I needed to get to his side immediately, and ultimately after his passing, I just needed to get home. During the craziness of that day, the story of Tamar entered my mind with emphasis on her returning to her father's house.

Returning to your father's house, which I refer to as returning to your people, can apply on several levels. In my case, it meant starting a job search that would allow me to sleep in my own bed every night. It also meant returning to Houston where most of my family, extended family, and friends that I grew up with could support me. For me, *return to your people* meant reconnecting with people who knew me prior to my marriage. Being immersed in an environment that shaped me helped me sort through and determine what aspects of the plans Marvin and I made together still fit me. I needed the nurturing and support of my family and friends.

Returning to your people can also mean identifying a tribe that enriches your life. Returning to your roots of singing, writing, running, or whatever interests you held in your youth will allow you to find people with those shared interests and promote rediscovery of yourself. In finding my tribe, I rediscovered my passion for writing.

What did you do before you were married that gave you joy? What is something you did that you couldn't be paid to stop doing? Now, more than ever, is the time to nurture yourself with self-care and self-soothing activities that promote internal peace.

Naomi
Ruth 1:6

She then made ready to go back to the plateau of Moab because word reached her that the Lord had visited his people and given them food.

Naomi lost her husband and two sons, which I imagine was devastating for her. She *required* a change in her environment just to have her basic need for food met. Therefore, she returned to her hometown among her kinsmen to meet that need. As we know, no one owes you anything, but you are more likely to find favor among your family. Even in her grief, Naomi found the strength to make decisions for herself and her family. She made the decision for herself, and her daughters-in-law, Orpah and Ruth, to pack up and move. Initially, her plan was to send her daughters-in-law back to their families. However, she also accepted they were grown women who could do what they pleased. Ultimately, Orpah returned to her people and Ruth stayed with Naomi.

Having two grown sons, this was an important lesson for me. For so long, my parenting involved telling them what to do and making decisions for them. Now, as men, I can advise them but ultimately, their decisions are their own. Like Naomi who advised Ruth on how to interact with Boaz, I am learning how to step into the mentor role and advise my sons. It is my advice to offer, but it is for my sons to accept or reject it.

Ruth
Ruth 1:17
> *Wherever you die I will die, and there be buried.*
> *May the Lord do so and so to me, and more besides,*
> *if aught but death separates me from you!*

As a young new widow, you have the power to choose every aspect of your life. It can feel overwhelming yet simultaneously, empowering. Compromise is part of every marriage and now you are in a new state of being. Ruth shows us that in addition to choosing where we live, we also can choose who we keep in our lives. Ruth chose to keep Naomi in her life. She chose to follow Naomi's advice concerning working in Boaz's field and their courtship.

As I stated before, home and family are terms you will define for yourself. Since Marvin's death, there have been people that have exited my life by choice, the way Orpah exited Naomi's and Ruth's lives. In those instances, the connecting factor was Marvin and since he is gone, it didn't make sense to have them stay in my life. On the flip side, there are people whose lives I have exited by choice. Again, in most cases, Marvin was the glue that bound us, so those relationships did not enrich my life anymore. One resounding lesson is you are free to leave people's lives without guilt.

The other lesson is to invite new people and new experiences in. While Bethlehem was home for Naomi, it was a foreign land for Ruth. As a married woman in those times, it was also likely she'd never worked outside the home. Now she was working in the fields as a gleaner to provide for herself and Naomi. The only way to grow and build your new identity is seek new experiences and remain open to having new people enter your life.

Ruth 11:12
All those at the gate, including the elders, said, "We do so. May the Lord make this wife come into your house like Rachel and Leah, who between them

*built up the house of Israel. May you do well in
Ephrathah and win fame in Bethlehem. With the
offspring the Lord will give you from this girl, may
your house become like the house of Perez, whom
Tamar bore to Judah.*

Did you notice that Israel and Tamar are
mentioned in Naomi and Ruth's story? The bottom
line—your life is not over. You are not defeated. You
will prosper and go on to accomplish great things for
yourself and your family.

These four people are not the only widows in the
Bible, but they served as the foundation I needed to
keep putting one foot in front of the other each day.
Even years later, I continue to revisit these passages
and get more meaning and more direction from them.
In addition to their examples, two other themes also
emerged: keep your ear to the street and change your
environment.

KEEP YOUR EAR TO THE STREET

The reoccurring advice is to return to your people, but it is not to become a recluse or a hermit. Tamar heard that her father-in-law, Judah, had come to town. Using that information, she devised a plan to hold Judah accountable to her as the widow of his son. Hence, she got pregnant and became an ancestor of Jesus, one of only five women mentioned in the genealogy of Jesus (Matthew 1:1-16). Naomi also kept her ear to the street. She heard there was food in Bethlehem which prompted her to leave Moab. Her decision led to Ruth also being listed in the lineage of Jesus.

The point is to fight the urge to collapse and stay down. Get up and get out, even when you don't feel like doing so. Keep your eyes and ears open so you don't miss opportunities that are presented to you. It's not enough to just hear things—you have to act on them. As we've been taught, faith without work is dead (James 2: 14-26). Every widow mentioned so far has done something. You are going to have to *do* something, too. The only thing guaranteed is change. You've experienced the ultimate change in going from married to widowed. Now you have to *do* some things…whether you like it or not.

CHANGE YOUR ENVIRONMENT

All of these widows moved, but you don't have to buy a new home or move to a new city. You will, however, need to make changes in your home if you are not moving. When my grandfather died, my grandmother got busy having rooms painted and furniture rearranged or replaced. She said we had to change the house so his spirit wouldn't recognize it and would move on. Otherwise, he would want to stay there with us. I don't know how true that was but I know the changes I made had a profound effect on me.

First, I got busy donating all of Marvin's clothes, shoes and hats. They needed to go because they contributed to me being stuck in anger. The house looked like he could walk through the door at any minute and that wasn't mentally healthy for me. As I removed Marvin's belongings, I had opportunities to reminisce over our years together. As with any marriage, we had good days and bad days, so depending on what I was handling and the memories attached to those items, I experienced happiness, sadness, joy, anger, every emotion in between, and ultimately, forgiveness. I had to forgive Marvin for leaving me even though death was not in his control. I had to forgive him for not giving me my happily ever after, and I had to forgive him for not allowing us to grow old together. Forgiveness, I learned, is accepting that the situation or circumstance turned out differently than what we expected and being okay with that. Please meditate on what forgiveness means to you. Then meditate on the phrase, "My home will rise up to meet me."

A YEAR OF FIRSTS

From the day your husband dies until the first anniversary of his death, you will have what I call a *Year of Firsts.* These are special days like holidays, anniversaries, birthdays, and other special occasions you will experience without your husband for the first time.

Marvin died in April, so my *Year of Firsts* started almost immediately with Mother's Day, Father's Day, my youngest son's prom and graduation, and Marvin's birthday which is July 16. None of this was easy to get through. They serve as reminders that you are alone and all the traditions surrounding those occasions have abruptly come to an end.

Thanksgiving was especially hard because Marvin was the person who fried turkeys for us and our neighbors. His absence was felt on our entire block because for years, he and the men on our street started gathering the night before to set up the fryer and just hang out. I injected the turkeys with seasoning and Marvin would take over from there. The first Thanksgiving without Marvin was sad for everybody.

My birthday is November 28 and that year, I chose not to celebrate my birthday at all. I attended a girlfriend's boat party since her birthday is November 30, but I did not call any attention to my own because it felt foreign. As my plus one, I took a long-time male friend so I would not be the only unattached person there. I also didn't want anyone's pity for my circumstance.

Then came Christmas. When I woke up on Christmas Eve, I realized I had not bought a single present, nor had I put up my Christmas tree. I was lying in bed giving myself a morning pep talk.

"Act like you have some sense," I told myself.

The message was two-fold. Pretend (act) like you have holiday cheer to bring a sense of normalcy back into our home, and take steps (act) to put up the tree and get out to get a few gifts. Once I put the tree up, then returned with gifts to put under the tree, my sons were inspired to get out and get a few gifts, too. While the amount and quality of the gifts weren't up to the standards of the past, it was a monumental accomplishment for our family.

After the high of *acting* like I had sense on

Christmas Day came the low of our wedding anniversary on December 27. That day opened a floodgate of emotions that drove me to our wedding pictures, followed by other pictures of our early years together. As the Bible says, "Count it all joy." Yes, I was hurting but I had to acknowledge the good that came out of our marriage. We were blessed with two sons, blessed with businesses, blessed with our home, and all the family trips we took over the years. The good outweighed the bad. So again, I got myself out of bed, cooked a big breakfast for myself, and moved forward.

The last of my *Year of Firsts* included New Year's Eve, New Year's Day, Valentine's Day, and Easter. New Year's Eve and Valentine's Day are days society tells us we need a love interest. Who are you going to kiss at midnight on New Year's Eve? Who do you exchange cards with and go to dinner with on Valentine's Day? Depending on what you normally did, these days can be especially difficult to get through. They are reminders of your change in status.

Luckily, Easter had always been my favorite holiday and I had lots of pleasant pictures and memories attached to it. I always made Easter baskets for the boys and Marvin throughout the years and had started to do so for my niece, too. Easter seemed to bring me back to myself. In addition to Christ's resurrection, that first Easter seemed to resurrect my internal joy. It had been a difficult year filled with ups and downs related to Marvin's death as well as other things that just come with day-to-day life. However, my zest for life was back.

We have choices related to staying in our sadness or moving into peace. During our marriage, Marvin lost both of his parents on the same day (on his birthday). I saw him succumb to grief and get stuck in anger at times. While he was going through that, I could not relate to his desire to stay on the couch on holidays instead of joining us for dinner. So, when I was faced with my own despair, I remembered how helpless I felt knowing I could not pull Marvin out of his anguish. I also did not want death to rob me of my potential for current happiness. I chose to move into peace.

When I was single and even early into my marriage, I used to collect quotes. Some time after Marvin's death, I restarted the practice and one of the first quotes I wrote down and meditated on was, "I am at peace with what was and welcome what's next!" As the anniversary of Marvin's death came and passed, that quote continued to give me strength as it does today.

Take some time to meditate on this: I am at peace with what was and welcome what's next.

* * *

If I knew then what I know now, I would have extended more grace to myself. Prior to my husband's death, I used to meditate on the quote, "You get points for trying!" That quote served me for most of my marriage and motherhood because it helped me to persevere and muscle through things when I was out of my comfort zone. As a mother of two boys after having grown up without brothers, I was out of my comfort zone at the beginning of each new phase of their lives. I was also out of my comfort zone in supporting Marvin when he was growing his business. So, I would push through and give myself a pat on the back for giving it my all. However, I did not realize that approach was detrimental when dealing with the year of firsts.

There were days I KNEW would be difficult emotionally, but instead of extending grace to myself by taking those days off or giving myself a slow start, I would jam-pack my day with meetings and tasks to avoid my feelings. But guess what? The minute I had a moment to myself, I'd breakdown and lose it. At a point near the end of my first year, I went to bed one night meditating on the word *forgiveness* and its meaning regarding myself and others, and I had a breakthrough that started at 1 AM in the morning. I use the term breakthrough because although I cried for twelve hours straight, it turned things around for me.

All the feelings and thoughts I had avoided bubbled up and out of me. At 1 PM, I was sitting in my backyard, completely cried out and felt that was enough. There weren't any more tears left to cry in that moment. Breakthroughs are messy and draining, but necessary.

So, I've gotten rid of the quote, "I get points for trying" and have replaced it with, "I love myself fiercely, loyally, and unapologetically." If I had known that quote then, I would have been loyal to me and given myself time and space to FEEL.

Be willing to sit in your feelings and ride them out because avoiding them only prolongs the hurt, and the hurt can manifest itself in unproductive ways in other areas of your life.

As you experience your *year of firsts*, pay attention to your physical, emotional, spiritual and mental health in the weeks and days leading up to those dates. Are you anxious? Are you irritable or find that your attention span has shortened? Please extend grace to yourself in the form of slow starts in the mornings, pampering baths or showers, a favorite candle scent, frequent breaks, short walks, journaling, or other activities that soothe you. As you continue through the year, you will learn what centers you and restores your peace.

TALKING TO GOD

Isaiah 54: 6 – 8

The Lord calls you back, like a wife forsaken and grieved in spirit, A wife married in youth then cast off, says your God. For a brief moment I abandoned you, but with great tenderness I will take you back. In an outburst of wrath, for a moment I hid my face from you; But with enduring love I take pity on you, says the Lord, your redeemer.

This scripture reminds me of the typical ebbs and flows found in marriage. Sometimes a husband and wife need space from each other, but when they come together again, they treat each other with tenderness. This scripture gave me the confidence to talk to God in my authentic voice. I did not have to use lofty words or perfect phrases in my prayers or make them long. It gave me the confidence to talk to God with the intimacy established by frequent and consistent communication found between a husband and wife, knowing that He will never leave me.

We have been taught to bring everything to God in prayer (Philippians 4:6-7) and that is exactly what I did. One Friday night, about four or five months after

Marvin died, a girlfriend of mine and I went to my neighborhood bar just to catch up since it had been a while since we'd seen or talked to each other. When we got there, the place wasn't crowded, but it was a lively mix of men and women. We walked in and sat at the bar. As my friend and I chatted, a man approached us and started flirting. I wasn't in the mood and quickly said a short, silent prayer to God.

"Lord, please keep men from approaching me tonight. They will ask if I'm married, and if I say I'm a widow, the conversation will go downhill fast and everyone will be depressed. If I say I'm single, it will sound like I'm inviting him to continue flirting and that's not what I want."

It was a very quick prayer, as if talking to my friend instead of God. My girlfriend and I continued talking for about ten minutes more and she stopped abruptly and asked, "Wait, is this a lesbian bar? Where are all the men?" I looked around and all the men were gone. Even the DJ was a woman and the bartenders were, too. God is listening! God listens and looks out for you.

Leaning on God as my husband, my prayers have become a bit more relaxed than they had been before. Marvin was my friend, and regardless of what we were going through, we found ways to laugh through it all. Our conversations weren't always deep and bordered on silly at times. Inevitably, one of us would say, "You're crazy!" I don't trivialize my prayers, however, praying several times a day has established a familiar feeling that I appreciate.

You will have highs and lows throughout your days. Some will be related to the grief you experience, and others will be byproducts of everyday life. In May 2019, a year into my widowhood, I started writing statements of gratitude at the end of each day. That is a practice I continue to this day. Daily statements of gratitude keep you motivated to keep moving forward. If you write them in the morning, they jumpstart your day. If you write them in the evening, like I do, they lift your spirits and end your day on a high. These statements of gratitude allow me to express appreciation for people and things I encountered that day. More importantly, it allows me to see firsthand how God listens and answers my prayers.

No matter how you do it, talk to God regularly and express gratitude daily. You will be surprised how fast you move out of denial and anger and toward acceptance of the new life you are building.

LIVING THROUGH
LONELINESS

Loneliness comes with widowhood. You *will* experience it regardless of your stage of grief. The five stages of grief are denial, anger, bargaining, depression, and acceptance. Right away, you will notice you're sleeping alone. The familiarity of his snoring, cuddling, or tossing and turning and your reactions to those things will be gone immediately.

You will also recognize that your routines no longer fit your lifestyle anymore, even though you desperately want them to. You will only need to make one cup of coffee instead of two, and the number of eggs for breakfast will reduce. These constant reminders magnify your loneliness. It also did not help that I was an empty nester. Both boys were away in college.

Marvin and I had several sets of matching coffee cups. Some were identical and others were themed, such as Mickey and Minnie Mouse. It was a way of adding some fun to our weekends. Marvin made the coffee on Saturdays and Sundays and used to bring them into the bedroom—a little too early for my taste. I'd be on the cusp of waking up when he'd say, "Good morning," in a melodious way followed by a peck on the lips. I'd always think to myself, "Why so early?!" but would scoot upward to a sitting position to take the coffee. We'd find something to watch on tv before jumping into our day.

Because of that, weekends were especially hard for me. Eventually, I stopped cooking altogether because it seemed easier to go out for meals. However, one Sunday at my parents' home, I developed a massive headache that would not go away. It hurt to even move my head. My mother pulled out her blood pressure machine and my blood pressure was through the roof. Meanwhile, I had never had any issues with high blood pressure before. Marvin used to check mine when he monitored his and always asked, "How do you keep ice water in your veins?" So, having a high blood pressure reading was scary. I was in the doctor's office the next morning describing my symptoms, and the first thing my doctor asked was, "Are you eating out regularly?" I answered, "Yes, because cooking just depresses me. It makes me feel lonely." He said, "You're going to have to cook your own food."

In Isaiah 54:6–8, I believe the words *abandoned* and *hid my face from you* are used because God is acknowledging to us that he knows we feel lonesome. At times during widowhood, we view ourselves as abandoned. Even though people will call and check on you, schedule brunch and dinner dates with you, and visit, the intimacy of your relationship with your husband cannot be replaced. The hugs and kisses, the phone calls about nothing during the day, and other routines the two of you established are gone. Touch is a human need, and widows are not being touched.

* * *

I have always enjoyed a glass of wine or a mixed cocktail, but as I sat back and paid attention to my feelings, I noticed that drinking made my loneliness worse. It took me two and a half years to realize. So, when I was out with friends and drinking socially, I was okay, but when I got home, the loneliness was too much to handle. Recently, very recently, I reduced my drinking because the weight of the loneliness was not worth the short-term relief alcohol gives.

During some of your loneliest moments, think back to what you were doing prior and identify your triggers. Were you drinking alcohol? Were you cooking? When you know your triggers, you can brace yourself for what follows and use coping skills. In the case of drinking alcohol, setting limits was better for me in the long run. Now when I drink alcohol, I only have moderate amounts and have a plan for activities with others following the drinks so I don't go home and sit with my feelings immediately afterward. Other times, I opt for mineral water with lime over ice as a mocktail instead of alcohol to socialize.

In the case of cooking, I found new ways of doing it to infuse fun. Initially, I signed up with a home delivery service that sent a box of ingredients for two with the recipes. The recipes I chose were usually outside of my cultural cooking, so it became an adventure. I'd have the leftovers for lunch the next day. Eventually, I cancelled the subscription and returned to some of my favorite childhood recipes but I cooked less of it and plated it so it was beautiful as well as nourishing.

What habits do you have that contribute to your loneliness? Can you remove those habits? If not, how can you change them so they serve you well and inject some joy?

BUILDING THE CONFIDENCE TO BE HAPPY AGAIN (RESILIENCE)

Isaiah 54: 11 -12

O afflicted one, storm-battered and unconsoled, I lay your pavements in carnelians, and your foundations in sapphires; I will make your battlements of rubies, your gates of carbuncles, and all your walls of precious stones.

E ntering widowhood is akin to entering a storm. As the scripture says, you are storm-battered. A visual representation is walking against hurricane-strength wind in thick mud while prickly, sideways rain pummels your face and body. Using my biblical imagination again, I envision a widowed woman opening her front door ashen, tired, and unconsoled to a beautiful view of sapphires, rubies, and other precious stones. But this storm-battered woman and these fine jewels just don't go together. One must change in order for them to match. It is easier for the woman to get herself together than for the pavement, foundation, and walls to be removed.

God is telling you in this scripture, as he told me, that better days are ahead. Those precious stones represent what God has for you, but you must get yourself together and be ready to receive it. In addition to receiving it, you must be prepared to enjoy it. What good is it to have rubies, sapphires, and other precious stones if you are not going to enjoy them?

Prior to my husband's death, I dressed appropriately for work, but in my free time and on weekends, I could be found in yoga pants, a t-shirt, and tennis shoes or flip flops. Also, as the mother of two young adult sons, I did not have a teenaged daughter pushing me to stay in style. It was a very slippery slope for me to look a mess when I didn't have anywhere to go. Guess what happens when you look in the mirror while already looking a mess? It makes you feel worse.

Like the woman in my biblical imagination, I had to take Naomi's advice to Ruth and bathe, anoint myself with oils and perfumes, then put on my best attire even when I did not feel like it. Then I had to do it again and again daily. If you are like me, the more you like what you see when you look in the mirror, the better you feel. The better you feel, the more confidence you gain.

God's promise to Ruth was fulfilled through Boaz, but I'm not sure she could have executed the instructions given to her by Naomi without the confidence she gained from cleaning herself up and refreshing her appearance. God's promise for you may not be fulfilled through a man, but it might be a business, a job, or something else that requires you to take bold, confident steps. Look like you want it and look like you are ready to enjoy it. What are you seeking that requires confidence to get?

You might be wondering why I needed confidence to be happy again. Mourning is personal and looks different from one person to the next. As a naturally optimistic person, it felt foreign to live in anger and grief. That led me to counseling. I attended my therapy sessions every two weeks and expressed LOTS of emotions through a plethora of exercises my therapist pulled out of her toolbox. As my anger diminished and my gratitude for the people and things that were still in my life increased, I looked happier. Yet, there were some people who told me I didn't look sad enough. My response was that God blessed me with twenty years of marriage and two amazing sons who I love dearly, and that our good days outnumbered our bad days, so sadness did not fit me anymore. Nor did I need to put my grief on display for others to see. I felt judged so I decided to dismiss their expectation for perpetual gloom and sadness, and choose instead to live. It took confidence in myself and my authentic feelings to dismiss their judgement and dismiss them from my life.

There is another widow in the Bible, Bathsheba, who dealt directly with societal customs associated with mourning. Let's take a closer look at her because there are some things we can learn from her, too.

Bathsheba
2 Samuel 11: 26-27

> *When the wife of Uriah heard that her husband had died, she mourned her lord. But once the mourning was over, David sent for her and brought her into his house. She became his wife and bore him a son. But the Lord was displeased with what David had done.*

As the scripture tells us, Bathsheba mourned her husband Uriah for the appropriate amount of time. The appropriate amount of time was based on societal and cultural norms. When the mourning period ended, she married David.

Bathsheba was a pregnant widow who publicly mourned the death of a man she cheated on, then married the man she cheated with. Placing ourselves in Bathsheba's shoes for a minute, imagine how she was very likely judged by everyone she encountered. Even if they did not say it to her face, they were thinking it and saying it behind her back. She may have even struggled with self-judgement, too, related to emotions such as guilt, shame, humiliation, or embarrassment. However, she moved past others' judgement because she went on to become Solomon's mother and another one of the five women listed in the genealogy of Jesus.

There were things wrong in Bathsheba's and Uriah's marriage. She committed adultery and he chose to stay among his soldiers rather than go home to his wife. In my biblical imagination, it may have been her loneliness that made her susceptible to lust which led her to adultery in the first place. She and Uriah were not a perfect couple in a perfect marriage. However, her peers relaying the story to others probably focused on her sins and gave Uriah pseudo-sainthood. That is why as widows we have to be careful of whose counsel we accept because if we accept counsel from a judgmental person, we can find ourselves stuck in mourning and wondering what we could have done differently.

STAY SAVVY

L ike the widow that dealt with the creditor, you will deal with people who truly believe your husband owed them something. On the day your husband died, he had friends, acquaintances, business partners or coworkers, and extended family. Although you would not think of these people as creditors in the traditional sense, if they approach you claiming your husband owed them money or a favor, they are creditors. You may have experienced this already, but if you have not, do not be surprised when it happens.

Only you know the specifics concerning your finances, but others will speculate. Some people will make the claim as a phishing exercise. Others will genuinely believe you owe them something. Unless you signed on the dotted line with your husband, or the debt stands in the way of you physically taking possession of property that belongs to you, then his debt was his and not yours. I am not a lawyer, but I know I must sign for things for them to become my responsibility.

The widow of 2 Kings 4:1-7 did not act hastily. She thought about who to go to for help, then took the time she needed to locate Elisha. That doesn't mean she didn't feel pressure or anxious about her situation, but she did not act hastily. She also took time to determine what she had to sell, solicit jars from neighbors for the oil, and then find buyers. She took her time to make each move her best move. Do not let nontraditional creditors push you into making hasty decisions regarding your money.

If you decide someone lacks a credible claim, simply say *no*. It takes confidence to say no and it takes strength to stick to it. No can sound like, "Oh, that is unfortunate," or it can sound like, "I'm not paying that." The situation and the person will determine the type of no you use. Then there will be times when a person has a credible claim but very poor timing. In general, anyone who came to me for money during the first six months of my husband's death is no longer in my life. Frankly, if they could not see my need for peace and understanding and chose to express their greed as a priority over my grief, they were not fit for my life. There was no coming back from that for me, so I chose to part ways.

* * *

As people make their claims, never agree in any way. For instance, someone may say, "I loaned Jerry $50 and never got it back. Wouldn't you want your money back?" This type of question could lead you to respond with a *yes*, which may lead the claimant to continue pressing the issue. Instead, respond in a noncommittal way like, "I hate that happened to you. I wasn't there so it seems that was between you and Jerry." Trust and believe you will be referred to as selfish, cold, heartless, and even a bitch, but at the end of the day, you still have your money. Regardless of what others may think, it is okay to safeguard your financial future and/or that of your child(ren).

Once you know a person is in the creditor role, you get to decide how much access they have to you. Because of technology, we can save phone numbers any way we like in our cell phones. Several people are listed in my phone by name followed by DNA or "do not answer." Occasionally, I take those calls just to keep my ear to the street and stay abreast of what is brewing. However, I do so when I am in the mood to deal with it. I have even had people show up on my doorstep, as if I would be intimidated into giving them money. Unless you live in a gated community where visitors can be turned away, you need to display decisiveness and fearlessness. Stick by your decision to disregard the claim, and communicate fearlessness by repeating your *no*.

Ultimately, you must decide whose will is bigger and act accordingly. If their persistence and tenacity intimidate you, their will is bigger. If your *no* stays consistent and you constantly display fearlessness, eventually the nontraditional creditors will back off making your will bigger. When you decide your will is bigger, stick to it without wavering, and pray about it without ceasing. Know you will come out of the situation(s) the victor.

RAISING CHILDREN

Isaiah 54:13

*All your sons shall be taught by the Lord, and great
shall be the peace of your children.*

Every widow is not a mother, but those who are
may feel the added pressure of navigating
your children through this difficult time. This
verse in Isaiah 54 was the second promise I stood on
after accepting God as my husband. Although my sons
were eighteen and twenty when my husband died,
they still needed parenting. In fact, they needed more
parenting than they ever had before because they were
dealing with the growing pains of transitioning into
manhood, as well as handling their grief. They, too,
were struggling, each in his own way. So, knowing
they <u>shall</u> have peace has been what I count on daily.
This verse does not say they will not be tested but I
have the assurance of God that they will be alright. In
fact, Isaiah 54:15–17 tells us that attackers will fail,
weapons formed against you shall not prevail,
accusations against you will be disproven, and the
Lord himself will vindicate you.

I continue to take comfort in all of this because my
children are my greatest blessing, as yours probably are
to you. The worst attack toward me is an attack against

my children. So, when trials pertaining to them do come, I absolutely stand on this word. I know they will be okay and have peace.

SOMETHING DIFFERENT, SOMETHING NEW

There is no shortage of catchy sayings on Instagram, Facebook, and the other social media platforms. However, two have stood out for me. "Old keys can't open new doors," and "You have to do something different to get something different," are my go-to mantras now. You cannot live in the past. You must move forward. Moving forward will look different for each of us.

Marvin died when I was forty-eight. As I was approaching fifty, I decided to give myself at least fifty new experiences. These would be my new keys to new doors. It took me about two years to learn this lesson, but having new experiences is really the only way to move forward. First, I got a passport. Then I found a travel buddy. As I said, God uses people to bless you and uses you to bless others. We found a reputable travel agency, decided on a nine-day tour of Italy from Venice to Rome, and booked it.

Planning and paying for that trip felt abstract until

it was time to pack and go to the airport. Then fear set in. Thoughts like, "Who do you think you are to take such an extravagant trip?" and "Why am I doing this?" were just two of hundreds of questions racing through my mind. Then I reminded myself of the sayings, "Old keys can't open new doors," and "You have to do something different to get something different." Find sayings or mantras that work for you. Find ones that will dispel fear, quiet doubts, and keep you moving forward.

I also joined clubs and committees I had never considered before, and I bought Amazon, Netflix, and other stocks that have given me firsthand lessons, too. I was even a co-host on a radio show once. When people invite you to an event, say *yes* and go. If there are things that intrigue you and you can ask to be included, do so. You will be surprised how often people say, "Yeah, come on!"

Another new key was a month of celebrating my 50th birthday. As I said, I did not acknowledge my 49th birthday. Because of that, I think my family and friends were equally committed to making sure I celebrated such a major milestone. As a result, I was gifted a wine party, a paint party, and a Thursday night happy hour. I co-hosted a dual birthday bash with my close dear friend that featured tiered cakes, balloon arrangements, and everything else you can think to have at a birthday celebration.

MOVING FORWARD

Earlier I introduced you to well-known widows in the Bible, however, there is one more worth mentioning. I saved her for last because each widow must decide for herself if and when she will date again. Like Ruth and Bathsheba, dating and marriage is a possibility if that is what you desire.

<u>Abigail</u>
1 Samuel 25:39

On hearing that Nabal was dead, David said: "Blessed be the Lord, who has requited the insult I received at the hand of Nabal, and who restrained his servant from doing evil, but has punished Nabal for his evil deeds." David then sent a proposal of marriage to Abigail.

I didn't start studying and meditating on Abigail until about two and a half years into my widowhood. Abigail's whole story is in 1 Samuel 25. When she is first introduced, she is still married and described as intelligent and attractive. We know she is intelligent by the way she took charge of the situation to reestablish peace between her husband, Nabal, and David. I imagine her intelligence enhanced her beauty, causing her find favor with David. Upon hearing of

Nabal's death, David sent for Abigail with a marriage proposal which she accepted.

Nabal was sick for ten days, but we don't know how long it took for word to reach David that he had died. However, Abigail stayed on David's mind and in his heart, and she desired to move forward with her life. Let's unpack this a bit as several lessons are found between these verses.

First, she was married to a man wealthy in livestock, land, and servants so she was accustomed to a certain lifestyle. Her husband Nabal, although feared by some and disliked by others, was someone that most looked upon as worthy of his stature in the community. So, when Abigail accepted David's proposal, she accepted his lifestyle and stature as well. She maintained her wealth and respect yet gained a loving godly partner instead of another wealthy fool.

Abigail taught me that in looking at future love interests, to level up. She went from a wealthy and respected man to a wealthy, respected, godly future king. She leveled up. Wealth is not the primary deciding factor. Leveling up is about saying yes to a man who values everything that is uniquely you. In Abigail's case, it was her intelligence and her beauty. David experienced Abigail's intelligence and attractiveness. In my case, it will likely be my sense of humor and my optimism. For you, it might be your persistence and talent. We all have unique gifts that set us apart from others and those gifts will allow us to engage with others. As a widow, you have a choice about dating, and if you decide to do so, remember to level up. Regardless of your choice, keep moving forward.

MAKING PEACE

In general, life is a journey, and specifically as a young widow, your journey is just beginning. While endings can be hard, they are also new beginnings. Widowhood begins in pain but with intentionality and consistency, you can rebuild your life in the way that suits you best. The thing about a current situation is that it is always changing. There are gifts in your current situation that can be built upon to create your next situation. Take time to meditate on the following: *I use my energy to heal and transform.*

Honestly, I do not have all the answers, but I do encourage you to make a vision board. After the meditations you've done to this point, you have likely begun to get intuition-based glimpses of how life could be for you. I started with a vision board, and it illustrated three basic things: sleeping in my own bed every night, a passport, and an international trip. Shortly after making that first vision board, I got my passport, booked a trip to Italy, and got a job that does not require travel. A vision board is really a visual prayer that you can look at every day. It will push you take the steps to make those things happen. Start small and continue to utilize vision boards to keep you engaged in crafting your life the way you want to live it and moving forward.

My prayer for myself and for you is that we keep moving forward and recognizing our uniqueness and greatness in the process. Widowhood brings out your warrior traits, so know you are more than a conqueror (Romans 8:37–38). Nothing, not even death, can separate us from the love of God.

I would like to hear from you!
Connect with me to let me know how you are doing.
🐦 @smckinl1
📷 @drshelleymckinley